Black birds

African oystercatcher

Alpine chough

American coot

American crow

Asian Koel

Austral blackbird

Bare-faced ibis

Biak black flycatcher

Black heron

Black scrub robin

Black stilt

Brewer's Blackbird

Cape crow

Carrion crow

Caucasian grouse

Chopi blackbird

Common raven

Crested myna

Eastern jungle crow

Fish crow

Giant coot

Giant cowbird

Glossy flowerpiercer

Hawaiian crow

Helmeted curassow

Indian blackbird

Large-billed crow

Shiny cowbird

Spotless starling

Tamaulipas crow

Torresian crow

Turkey vulture

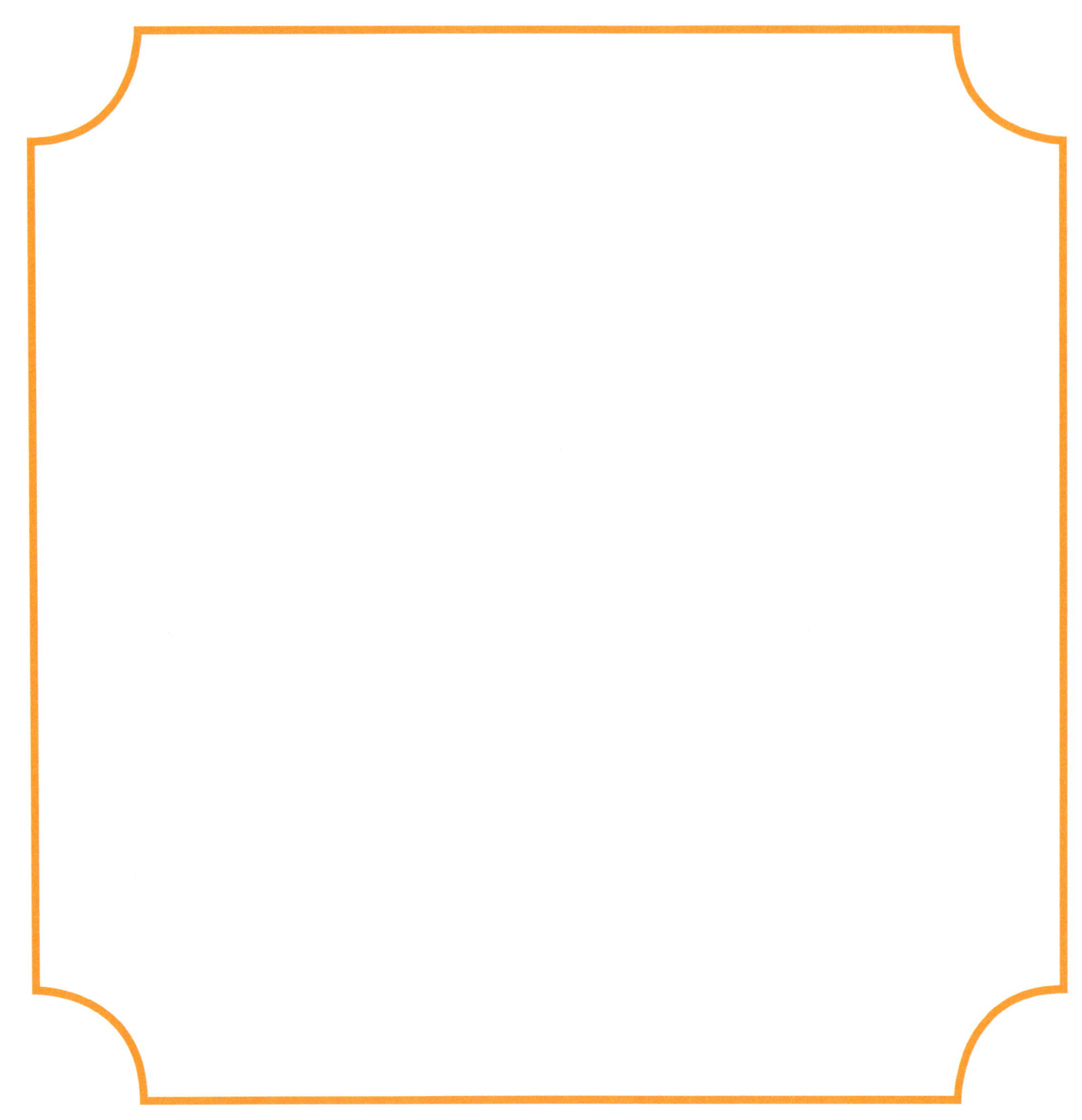

www.ingramcontent.com/pod-product-compliance
Lightning Source LLC
Chambersburg PA
CBHW041522070526
44585CB00002B/46